allostatic load

Also by Junie Désil and published by Talonbooks

eat salt | gaze at the ocean

allostatic load

poems

Junie Désil

Talonbooks

© 2025 Junie Désil

All rights reserved. No part of this book may be reproduced, stored in a retrieval system, or transmitted, in any form or by any means, including machine learning and AI systems, without the prior written consent of the publisher or a licence from Access Copyright (the Canadian Copyright Licensing Agency). For a copyright licence, visit accesscopyright.ca or call toll-free 1-800-893-5777.

Talonbooks
9259 Shaughnessy Street, Vancouver, British Columbia, Canada V6P 6R4
talonbooks.com

Talonbooks is located on xʷməθkʷəy̓əm, Sḵwx̱wú7mesh, and səlilwətaɬ Lands.

First printing: 2025

Typeset in Minion
Printed and bound in Canada on 100% post-consumer recycled paper

Talonbooks acknowledges the financial support of the Canada Council for the Arts, the Government of Canada through the Canada Book Fund, and the Province of British Columbia through the British Columbia Arts Council and the Book Publishing Tax Credit.

Library and Archives Canada Cataloguing in Publication

Title: Allostatic load : poems / Junie Désil.
Names: Désil, Junie, author.
Identifiers: Canadiana 20240455436 | ISBN 9781772016062 (softcover)
Subjects: LCGFT: Poetry.
Classification: LCC PS8607.E758275 A79 2025 | DDC C811/.6—dc23

To my love, Reza

I can't write about self-care without first pointing toward the obvious – your care cannot impede on the care of others. Just like the concept of freedom – ask yourself, is it really freedom if it is only for some?
—**FARIHA RÓISÍN**
Who Is Wellness For?: An Examination of Wellness Culture and Who It Leaves Behind (2022)

prologue I

searching for indicators
they palpate and trace the path of veins. run their index and middle fingers down my forearm.
sometimes slap, tap to awaken hiding, dormant veins. sometimes pull out a near-infrared technological device to illuminate my vasculature *for optimal peripheral venous access.*

laser-pointer red veins a map for the phlebotomist to orient the needle. blue, rubber tourniquet to increase blood pressure. now they will draw blood – look for an explanation – garnet coloured, filling the various tubes.

these trails of veins, this sanguine fluid transport system, health history carried in this circuitry of cells and plasma. they look for signs of chronic stressors – cortisol levels, elevated cytokines, c-reactive proteins. they look for markers of inflammation, metabolic markers like total cholesterol, albumin, triglycerides, and waist-to-hip ratio. they ask the typical questions about allergies while measuring systolic and diastolic blood pressure.

they want these diagnostics – i want the diagnostics – to provide enough clues to decipher cause.

but they fail to uncover the origins beneath.

Practitioners of modern medicine are not trained to be healers. They are trained to be biomedical technicians.
—**RUPA MARYA** and **RAJ PATEL**
Inflamed: Deep Medicine and the Anatomy of Injustice (2021)

part I

allosta

tic load

tidbit

wake up to this heart
hammering
for the attending it's been asking for
care
blood is under pressure –
to block
up the valves to your life's chamber

my lower back on fire
crawl out of bed

to the bathroom
call in sick

thought the pain was
the result of the new

old chair i had inherited.
for three days i crawled.

on the fourth, i walked
half bent over to a clinic

stressed about getting a note
for my absence.

the straight-up deluge of work
i would go back to.

the sterile glare of the grey-white fluorescents
casts a clinical pallor that envelopes the examining room. i hold my breath as the cuff squeezes, and a current of pain surges up my left arm gripping my neck. i pretend it's fine, even as the cuff pops open, generating an incomplete reading. after three different cuffs have been used to constrict my upper arm, and after the readings fluctuate wildly, each number higher than the last, this practitioner gives up – she'll get the doctor to manually check my blood pressure. i sit, embarrassed – my whole body smoulders while the nurse practitioner expresses concern – *are you on any medication to control it?* – about my borderline hypertension.

i swear up and down that it's fine, that this really only happens when i come into medical offices and hospitals. the cuffs are never the right size. they scramble looking for the proper cuff, adding another five to ten minutes to my appointment. while they scurry and confer out of earshot, but still in my line of sight, pointing and gesturing, my anxiety mounts.

a nurse practitioner bustles in with a new cuff, a wider band to accommodate my arm. i apologetically try to explain that doctors stress me out – the pressure on my arm increases – and so does work – the digital numbers climb – i stop myself from going into detail, stop myself from leaking all over the floor.

she says she'll pretend this number did not happen, gives me five minutes, and tries again. when she reads the numbers, her eyes behind gold-rimmed glasses close, as the corners of mine seep liquid salt. she offers to write me a note – *but talk to your doctor* – excusing me from work for three days – *to get more time.*

at work i'm asked to review policies
particularly
sick leaves and absenteeisms
quiet quitting and long-term leaves that turn into
resignations

review the anonymized data
on use of our benefits
find myself in the statistics
everyone is on some kind of
antidepressant to make it through the
find-myself days where we can't

find a woman and her five kids
housing while some live in precarity
waiting for the renoviction adjacent
to the *poorest postal code*
most of us are under pressure
medicating blood

the surveillance job
that monitors your presence
Dear _____,
this is to confirm that per
our last conversation on _____
you have been absent for
too many days, your employment
is in jeopardy i have weaponized
your underlying cause as reason
for this disciplinary letter

yours,
Management

in the doctor's office
i'm asked multiple times

if i have diabetes despite
my lab results showing

that i do not. the locum
looms, balances awkward

and belligerent confidence
stares at a point above my head

while i stare – above hers – at an
intricate poster of the heart muscle

another of fibrous ropy images of inside
musculature – lines lead to names

of organs: *when i look at you
and people of your ethnicity*

*i would say you should
start on Metformin.*

scrawls on her notepad she
tells me have *a think.*

feet dangle helplessly
from the examination table.

her exit as abrupt as her
entrance.

[get ready]
get up out of bed.
[get ready]
my heart is pounding
a steady,
[put on my left sock]
anxious drumbeat.
about to
[find the right sock]
start
my work commute,
[rummage slow for undies]
barely stepped out of the house
[right leg, that's it]
to drown out the pounding,
it
[left leg, in you go]
and the public transit
[find some bottoms – clean]
slurs
[right leg, you got this]
i wear loud pink earbuds jammed
[left leg, struggle, sciatic pain]
[shimmy awkwardly – painful – into the tights]
deep into
my ears
[grab black hoodie, ask for help to put it on]

this is how i can get to work:
drown out the daily (micro) aggressions
with Aretha Franklin's "Struggle,"
the remix version.

hood up to block out what
i already know will come –
thank you Aretha –
'cause I've got bills to pay.

in the ER room the doctor on duty
after
yelling
DO YOU KNOW WHAT YOU HAVE?!
after
informing me that i have
a pulmonary embolism
after
i look it up on my phone –
Serena Williams had one –
after
i don't finish reading the Wiki article
after
i soothe myself, think if an athlete,
the best in the world, mind you,
had one …
after
sticky pads are attached to my
gel-swabbed chest
after
the Doppler ultrasound probes
the inguinal crease
after
it glides along each thigh, down
around to my calf
after
it sends painless sound waves
after
numbing contrast dye
flows cold through my veins
after
i am glided through the CT
scanner
after
i am returned to ICU
where i am blasted full of thrombolytics

after.

i am left. breathless.

Any history of

mother's side: father's side:
stroke   diabetes

mother's side: father's side:
diabetes   stroke

breast cancer   cancer (which kind?)
ovarian cancer (maybe)   cancer (i don't know which)
cervical cancer (maybe, I don't know which)   cancer
hypertension   her heart seized
heartbreak   he suffered a great shock

saisie

                        just screen me then

                we would have to screen you routinely

manman tells me she has cancer
we make small
talk in circles. she asks about the
mundane like *do you pray*
when did you last read the Bible?

what she means is:

don't worry, you don't have to interrupt your life.
manman tells me she has cancer
a year after she is diagnosed
don't worry you don't have to

in between more questions,
now about my marriage, *are you happy*,
how is your health?
worrying me about her bills, her sons,
her failed dreams, her burdens.

my phone's glass screen
grows hotter, pressed
against my ear, think about
potential cancered waves
undulating out of the screen,
to make their earworm way
into my brain, spread their tentacles,
repose in the fatty folds of my brain.

she tells me –
in the closet tucked in behind
bolts of never-used fabric –
where to find
her important papers in case.

her anxieties about my soul's future
place in heaven
override my attempts to soothe
mine about her diagnosis.
what kind of
body-ravaging cancer is it,
how long should i come home –
where to pack and leave
my already uprooted suitcased life.

inheritance
the sibilant *S* lisp
faint rattle of your congested chest
tell me you're dying
ignore your words   wasted

conversations   a finality punctuated by the click
of the phone   line
held together by coiled thread
next
          conversation – death and dying

what is it like to prepare for
the inevitable

what remains unsaid
the weight of sadness
heiress to the burden
of persistent worry

how to
inherit joy where there is little
to bequeath

as he holds himself together
tries to hold his stomach together
sucks back Rolaids
papa's guts rotting

Pepto Bismol an aperitif and Phillips'
Milk of Magnesia – dessert,
while he sits hunched over the dining table

i often wonder about amnesia
when i remember his high-
effort coping

in the dining room that served as study
white lab coat kept him
warm

the ulcers make his breath foul
as he studies medical texts, bookmarked
by sheafs of perforated computer paper

lined green – spit out of the printer
the racist joke posted on the corkboard that
he'd take down at the end of the day

from the real estate office where he
worked. he has no recollection, though
when the doctor asked: *any stressors?*

he replied: *no.*

at work when i log in
my emails number in the three digits.
still. emerge from my four-day
migraine

and previous to that my two-week
vacation working-at-home-catching-up
staycation, and previous to that a number

of breaks that have done nothing
to bring my stress or workload down. i start
the twentieth to-do list

that never gets shorter
and my heart begins its erratic
thumping.

i read *goop*
what will Gwyneth Paltrow
tell *me*

make room in your schedule for
free time and activities that you truly love

start the day with a breakfast that helps
manage blood sugar levels

prioritize sleep

do your best to remove unnecessary
stressors

i read the health
and wellness articles, fantasize about
implementing some of the tips
to lower my stress

my mornings start
with phone screeches
alarm tones meant to
get me out of bed immediately
jump-start my sapped heart
caffeinated dopamine courses
through my nervous system
sugary-sweet pastry ensures
saccharine-joy high
sticks around –
long enough to get dressed
and head out the door.
so much for *goop*.
so much. for grace.

From: < >
Sent: Thursday, February 16, 2023, 11:15 a.m.
To: < >
Subject: RE: RE: strategic priorities

your email did not find me
well   your email instead has
found me

with a mountain of work
to do and
people need me.

they need me to do it.
the work i mean
i don't want to be needed.

i want to abdicate from responsibility
but i'm the cleanup crew
(if you know you know).

i read a debunked theory
that women with endometriosis
put their careers first

before themselves.
some theories persist. work
before health.

and here i am

signed,

All The Worst

on my Nth visit to yet another medical professional
when the medical-office assistant ushers me down the hall
and asks me to get on the scale
it fails to tell her that the number reflects
the cares i neglect to dispense,
emails i forgot to dispatch – including the ones sitting
rent-free in my brain, the owed return phone calls,
and text messages, and emails, and to-dos,
and 252 open tabs, and
unfinished conversations settling in my chest,
on my hips, in my thighs. i eat my feelings
because it's unacceptable to have them, no that's not
true. i portion control my emotions and keep
my mouth busy so as not to earn the *angry Black woman*
badge. the amount of viral headlines i ingest daily –
the ones with constant images of nooses
around our necks, the funeral pyres i build in
these heart chambers and the ashes that collect – cold
the oxygen i hold trapped in this ribbed
cage, the adipose tissues cradling the climate –
quotidian knife-tipped insults, slights,
pass overs, the *go back home* slurs
the *where are you (really) from* (not so innocent)
queries the subtext beneath the *your English is perfect
you're really smart* the *sorry this place has been rented*
or simply not answering the door – though i saw a hand
quickly part the pointelle white curtain – the *your paper
is too angry, too personal, not objective*, perhaps *plagiarized*.
i turn the other cheek, no the face, no the entire body as i
offer my back as a shield. still too much weight.
the medical office assistant scribbles the number in my file.

the woman who rested her thin silvered cap of hair died
that is when she rested her head it was
more permanent than i thought at the time.
i smiled inwardly at the ordinary vulnerability
of falling asleep on a stranger and hoped she
wouldn't overapologize for dying on me.

arrived at my work appointment late. embarrassed
at being late again. or rather cortisol-amped
that i couldn't sleep. i couldn't wake
without drowning in an ocean. i couldn't
put myself whole without being late.
i couldn't explain why

i was often late.
though when the woman who rested her thinning
silver-capped hair died, i was in fact on time.
or, would have been on time, but i rode two stops
further, afraid to wake her. afraid to endure
secondhand embarrassment at her cheeks sunken

like a deflated balloon.
mouth open, gums exposed.
i rode the bus to that job that
would make me leak all over the floor, that
would shamelessly rob my personal time, the job
that was not for profit, but where care was transactional

on my way to the job to train my successor
an older woman died on my shoulder. at
the bus stop i stood for some time immobile,
late again – castigate myself
i did not stay longer.

at the gynecologist's office
it's my second time.
the first time to determine
if i had endometriosis.
she sent me for a round of tests
instead of a laparoscopy
the *gold standard*
for an endometriosis diagnosis –
it's not necessary she told me.

this time
i wait patiently as she nibbles
a sandwich, mouse-like in the hall
directly across from the examination
room – from our shared lines of sight
through the door, she can see that
i can see her cutting
neatly into my appointment time
as she continues to eat.

this time
i'm in her office for an IUD,
as recommended by the ER doctor
following my embolism.
since i am actively trying to conceive
i am high risk
a high-risk pregnancy
i'm thirty-nine already
a geriatric pregnancy.

when she has dusted her hands
tidily, says *sorry i'm late*
as if she means it
tells me to *pause those*
plans. really? i don't say,
she already knows my age
and i stare at her bread-dusted
hands.

From: <   >
Sent: Tuesday, April 11, 2023, 16:54 p.m.
To: <   >
Subject: RE: RE: RE: RE: RE: RE: Performance

at work i am called a racial slur
look it up – you're in the dictionary
says the client.

at a health sector directors' meeting
no one will look at me
or talk directly to me even when i sit
at the head of the conference
table.

at another meeting crammed in a dark
corner of a near-empty pub, the smell
of filthy mop water and Pine-Sol
does not cover the fact that i am
constantly talked over.

i politely
ask the man to let me finish
as he has spoken at length and over me.
*i do not need a dressing down
by the likes of you,* he says.

in yet another meeting
i am told that *in an ideal world*
i would be handling *x y z*
in my work portfolio instead of
putting out fires.

i do not tell them all the things
i wouldn't be doing
in an ideal world.

smaller
in public. whittle self down. avoid spillover. compress self.
rearrange bones, muscles, adipose tissue. numbness creeps up.
can't feel the seat. even the right leg goes dead. moist breath, kiss
windows. confront reflection. make self smaller. avoid manspread.
or apologetic, make more space. still. i reshape like dough. still.
spread like dough.

when i was younger i'd walk myself thin. followed the curved
sidewalk to school and back. i couldn't run with the knives slicing
my shins. stabbing my lungs. i learned about girdles – beige ones
manman would wear with *spice coloured* pantyhose. clipped high
on her thigh, smoothing silhouette. i learned to wear them once a
week for church. then every day to make myself smaller.

i have discarded the daily ritual of sucking air. tucking and
rearranging my belly. dancing shimmy up, right down, up left
down, wriggle, yank! snap! of the elastic, lycra bands. gather
my flesh orderly smooth. compress skin, muscle against padded
bones. i have discarded the daily ritual of wearing a girdle.

have i told you that i have gotten cleverer at shapeshifting, folding
and moulding? now i sit still. so still as to disappear. my blood
slows itself, grows turbid and clots. so still. my calf charley horses.
clots claw up my leg, travel through veins, set up in my lungs.

the doctors look for reasons: *did you have any pain prior?* no.
did you previously experience shortness of breath? no. but i've
long held my breath. i sat too still. uncomfortable with asking for
a chair with more yield, space for my spreading flesh.

resignation letter with help from Hillary Leftwich and Sade
sometimes the sunrise looks better once it's behind you
in front – a pit better than hope

would you hold love
conditioned to the mistakes we've feasted

on, famished. only strings remain corded
to throats shredded mute

hearts divided, stoppered care
wash our conscience bleach-level clean.

you could eat your feelings off the floor of
performed care and be next to godliness.

and i would *disappoint my future if i stay*

prologue II

Coping Like John Henry

- I've always felt I could do what I want in my life.

- If I decide to do something, I stick with it until it's totally done.

- I like doing things other people thought impossible.

- Things not going as I want them to makes me work harder.

- Sometimes I feel I have to do something if it's to be done right.

- I typically find a way to do things I really need done, although it can be difficult.

- The results of my hard work rarely disappoint me.

- I am a person who stands up for what I believe in, no matter the consequences.

- Even when things get tough, I don't lose sight of my aims.

- I need to do things as I want to, rather than how others might want me to.

- I am not hindered by my personal feelings.

- Hard work has helped immensely to get ahead in life.

high-effort coping: subject matter for inspiration porn.

---

a fabled story for my condition.

---

something that will eventually kill you – a medical phenomenon.

---

named after John Henry Martin – no relation to the man in the ballad "Man vs. Machine."

---

vowed to beat the sharecropper system he was born into.

---

taught himself to read and write.

---

then freed himself and his children.

---

at forty-five he borrowed money to pay for his seventy-five-acre

---

parcel to pay down the loan.

---

farmed the land day and night

---

seven days a week, taking five years instead of thirty.

---

by his fifties: hypertension, arthritis, peptic ulcers so bad 40 percent of his intestines were removed.

---

not without struggle, and not without a price.

part II

weath

ering

forecast says 100 percent rain
eyes mirror the streaming windows

lie in bed – not even a cup of water – it's a bad pain day
i don't need them to hear the tremor

in my voice – should i email or
text that i can't come in

or force myself to work?
my back aches something fierce.

forecast calls for rain on end
incessant drip

wet coldness seeps thru exposed
wrists, ankles, behind fogged glasses

reflects bright screen, a digital tapestry of
pixelated death gone viral

back braced, teeth clenched, pelvis squeezed
white digits – triplets – encircled by red dots

testament to ignored messages.
i don't want to read performative horror

bookended between images
#nofilter

curated aspirational perfection

do not circulate

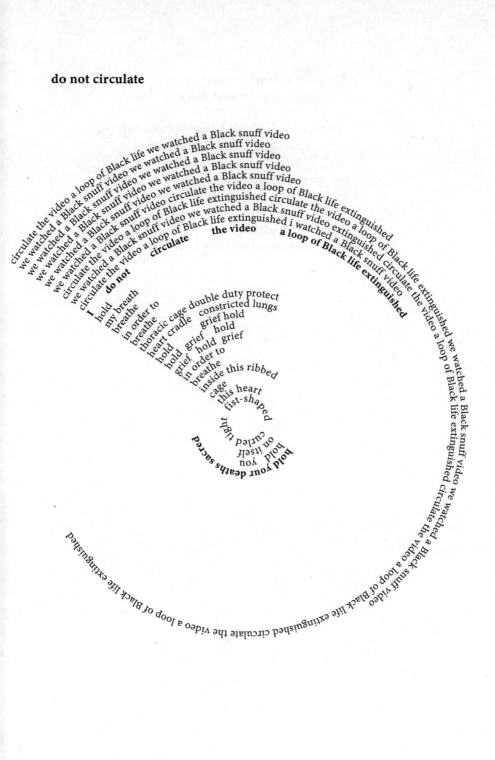

this body's weathervane
is an instrument turned this way

and that – sensing a climate pattern pointed
in the direction of bad winds to come.

the parts that creak, groan,
refuse to stretch – dangerously taut

and close to fracture.
some days are a good day to *call in Black*.

on a good day:
fatigue-fogged brain
only a dull ache
in my lower back and pelvis

on a particularly bad year-long stretch
of racial injustice, extrajudicial killings

work microaggressions
general climate of anti-Blackness

my body expropriated – pain
wouldn't let me out of bed

my body – was this betrayal? or
affirmation

the weather is bad out there
        in here the weather is bad

        out there the unceasing patter of rain erodes
   dampness lodges – settles

           erodes
           dampness lodges – settles
           rain

makes an awkward home in the joints
           muscles and inflamed tissues
   makes muscles and inflamed tissues
           a home – awkward in the joints

get up anyway brave the shifty climate
put on the
happy
face

the world wants to see

the world, even on sunny days
is filmy-grey

other days it's like looking through
a sobbing tear-tracked window

i'm asking those rays though
please make it possible to weather
i'm asking

the rest of the year

Patient Health Questionnaire

Over the last 2 weeks, how often have you been bothered by any of the following problems? (Use "✓" to indicate your answer)	Not at all	Several days	More than half the days	Nearly every day
1. Little interest or pleasure in doing things	0	1	2	3
2. Feeling down, depressed, or hopeless	0	1	2	3
3. Trouble falling or staying asleep, or sleeping too much	0	1	2	3
4. Feeling tired or having little energy	0	1	2	3
5. Poor appetite or overeating	0	1	2	3
6. Feeling bad about yourself — or that you are a failure or have let yourself or your family down	0	1	2	3
7. Trouble concentrating on things, such as reading the newspaper or watching television	0	1	2	3
8. Moving or speaking so slowly that other people could have noticed. Or the opposite – being so fidgety or restless that you have been moving around a lot more than usual	0	1	2	3
9. Thoughts that you would be better off dead or of hurting yourself in some way	0	1	2	3

since the skies darkened
and rain pierced through clouds

since the day's shadows
have lengthened

---

listless can't get up

---

my eyes leak wet warmth
soul feels heavy

---

mummified in my blankets

---

unintentionally simultaneously disinterested and obsessed.
when i wake i do a full 360

---

i practice intermittent fasting

---

turning leaden limbs and face another wall
guilt-strapped to the bed

---

i keep my book open, the TV on, my phone clutched in my
hand; i rewind the movie i watch for the eighth time, scan the
subtitles, scroll through Instagram

---

sometimes my words pour slowly off my tongue cold as molasses
dark and bitter   my fingers repeatedly knot and coil around
each other; i wear a worry path between the couch and bed

---

fantasize about how nice
it would be to not rouse my heart
murmur   just give up

doctor:
let's get some blood work done
start you on a subclinical dose
of citalopram
in a week you should start to
perk right up

instead
on the train watch
cherry blossoms whiz by
Thom Yorke's falsetto a
repeated reminder

this is fucked up, fucked up.
on a two-month down
in the sinkhole of depression
partially functional

listen to the beats drop
mournful angst on the playlist
i labelled *yt gal music.*
stored collection of downlifting

tempos on a loop   sway alongside
complicated loss
or in bed – cocooned sadness
the tired adage a counterbeat:

depressed folks see the world as is.
i'm certain the sheets have shifted
to accommodate the bed's depression
shaped by my skin and bones.

i've been a funk of pain.
stare at the ceiling   my artist's canvas
among the popcorn.
exhaled worries a surrealist vision

of where we're headed.
taught to turn away ghosts whose maws
gape open   shout warning:
our world is on fire.

i've collected tired selfish fears.
ash rains through closed fists,
forms charcoaled letters; perhaps
we'll read the signs first.

brain chatters frantically
reminds me of my long list of priorities and the breaths
i forget to take – deep and long and shuddering.

i could tell you about the baths i soaked in, not
long enough to prune – not long enough – steam still
rises from my skin, the bathroom a fog. the baths that
turn into infrequent showers.

i could tell you about the many candles i've lit
inhaling their supposed calm, the many incense sticks
i've burned. the litter of perfumed powder on tables
and windowsills – an offering to some deity of calm.

the soothing binaural beats, the deep chill, the focus,
the sleepy-time sirens, the ambient dreams, the drift away
indie, the rain sounds, ocean sounds, wind chimes – playlists.
and failing that, purchasing Calm only to listen to *Sleeping
Beauty* with Alan Sklar on repeat.

or the stolen forest walks, resentful promenades around
the seawall. avoid the steep steps of Grouse
but not the grinding gears of the non-profit.
at least it doesn't require physical fitness or prowess,
just heartbreak stamina.

meanwhile in the blue light
i research productivity everything
always at night download apps
each ping each reminder snooze
through supplements and i
swipe through drink water and
take my health reminders box
breathe and focus i discover
more apps that promise
time management

while the blue light that emanates
from my screen is slowly killing me

nightly i scroll through posts watch
many videos to learn to knit
to can to build an outhouse i
research the heck out of baking
bread and repurposing old furniture
i never do knit but my canning is
on point my sourdough is solid and
i do make flavoured cakes delicious
good texture yes a good crumb
moist but not too moist
but still not the fantastical ones
decorated with mounds of colourful
icing rosettes i would need
to fulfill my fantasy of running
a small bakery

instead i menu plan and practice
progressive relaxation and
somatic exercises and
read nutrition science in the blue light
and input my exercise and update
my period tracker and update my budget
in that grace period before the app
purported to help me save
charges me monthly

tethered to technology
in the pursuit of well-being
promised liberation from the chains
of poor habits
i am ensnared by the glow
of blue light

cancel Calm, and apps like Focus, Zen, and Freedom
the ones that liberate time.
close all the two hundred and fifty-two open
tabs on my phone about self-care, mindbodygreen,
sourdough recipes. listicles, *BuzzFeed*, *Bored Panda*,
20 FACTS ABOUT MARLON BRANDO
and other articles like "How I Stopped Working
for the Man and Brought In
over Six Figures a Month," says the rosy-cheeked
french-manicured blond influencer.

cancel all my health-type subscriptions,
turn off all my notifications and reminders
to drink water, to get up and stretch for thirty seconds,
to box breathe. cancel previously free now not-free pandemic
subscriptions during my short-lived shelter-in-place
aspirations of knitting, breadmaking, preserve making,
guitar playing, indie-film watching.

put on my noise-cancelling earphones
and actually – i want to so much –
rest

"Caring about" along axes of oppression and charity allows supremacies to re-create themselves surreptitiously. Part of colonialism's sleight of hand is its normalization of the capitalist political, economic, and ecological framework in which care is practised.
    —**RUPA MARYA** and **RAJ PATEL**
    Inflamed: Deep Medicine and the Anatomy of Injustice (2021)

Carewashing[1]

I

church. i remember the quarterly
humility service we participated in.
you were supposed to wash the feet
of your fellow congregant.
white-enamelled, blue-rimmed tub
filled with lukewarm water and
special, crisp-white linens draped
on shoulders.
my manman never picked friends
or maybe they didn't pick her
but she always washed the feet
of one of the two older white
women no one talked to.
she never wrinkled her nose at their bunioned
feet in cheap beige-coloured panty-
hose. perfunctorily, perhaps,
she would always – humility-pat
their feet.

II

secularly, we try to love each other
conditionally or for a paycheque,
make *something inherently relational
into something to be consumed like
a hamburger.*
an observation that as we are paid
to care, we care less for the folks dispensing
care – less for the folks in need and
we're all awful people surviving capitalism.
even without threat of hell and damnation
or implorations to love your neighbour
as yourself.

---

[1] Presenting ourselves as genuinely concerned about social or humanitarian issues using the language or imagery associated with care and compassion to distract from or mask unethical behavior, lack of substantive action, or harmful practices. —J. Désil

III
i can't remember who washed my feet
when i was old enough to partake
likely it was a friend and i don't remember
whose feet i washed – that time is a blur of
damnation trauma. i remember that it was Easter
weekend, and it was sunny and beautiful
for Winnipeg (*spring came in like a lamb*)
and that service was longer and the smell
of food warming, tickling our stomachs,
a potluck that we couldn't stay for.
the upswell of the organ and piano, and
voices lifted, as we cannibalized the body
of Christ the wafer Styrofoam-textured washed
down with Manischewitz wine.
but i did not know how to care unconditionally
how to have humility.

IV
in the morning when i have difficulty
caring for myself before i wrestle my
careworn heart to submission, so i can
grieve, be anxious, be solicitous
note the irony of being in service to the state's
offloading and feminization of labour
i remember my mother who quietly and simply
kneeled. soft hair black and shiny in a chignon
she pinned low to her neck.
back bent, Vaseline-glossed lips pressed
firmly among the row of bent-over women
scooping water over nyloned feet, in service
to the seated woman in front of her.

breath/breathe
chest weighted. holds oxygen close in the thoracic cage. over a year of guarded pain. trapped air – unable to circulate breath. that year in what passed as lockdown the birds were a cacophony in so-called New West, see clear to Surrey, from across the Fraser River at the *spot*.

which is to say the space between the church and the condo
where roof-shaking gospel would play the chorus swell and
(supposedly) take my doubts and breath away – in a month
the air in my lungs would be trapped between these bars of
unending grief – how to move on, carry on, live on, as the air is
repeatedly extinguished from your pulmonary cradle.

on the treatment bed the acupuncturist tells me to fill my lungs –
i (wrongly) presume to lessen the shock of the pinpricks – and
so i scoff internally and breathe deep shuddering breaths. needle
plunges in as air expels. what would you like to listen to? i always
say ocean – the roar of salt and water i imagine twinning the
blood's rush in my veins.

i am sometimes embarrassed by birds whose names i don't know. another time or perhaps, when i have another time, i might make their acquaintance. *hello, sorry I don't know your name.*

one's name i learn by accident when i find another time and space to sit and while cars parked under the awning of early COVID fear – for once not choking our lungs – unending stream of exhaust down highways. *Spinus tristis.*

i mention birds in the same breath as racial trauma. i remember finding an injured bird, its tiny chest heaving and fluttering and beating – wildly – that's how my chest has always felt. my whole life. i keep being told to just breathe even when pollutants and unshed grief battle to expectorate themselves from these lungs.

the birds in this patch of borrowed paradise are loud on the Zoom calls i take outside. i over-apologize *over* the sounds of the loud Pacific wren. i learned its name when i decided to download SmartBird ID and when later i apologize to Pacific wren for talking over them.

the air out here that i manage to draw in through the space between breath and grief is sweet and green-filled. the constant sound of trains screeching by, shaking the ground, forlorn whistles, covers the sound of highway traffic that has resumed after eight weeks of near silence. i forget that the world keeps spinning on itself. through the chaos, my lungs remember and anticipate smoke-filled summers in the valley below. summers filled with wildfires. lungs choked by particulates, halting my breath. exhausted, i'm on guard for the signs of blood clotting my lungs, travelling up my leg by way of these veins.

every year that i still breathe is a milestone. i've rosary counted seven bead-like years, calculating my risk for another pulmonary embolism. unprovoked PE the hospital called it *no recent surgery? no "recent trauma"?* just shortness of breath and the feeling of dying *no warning signs?* is the chest pain, alarming – a sign? feeling like i'm dragging myself? arrhythmic beats? just the stress of unrelenting violence on all life: shorted.

sometimes the sounds of cottonwood leaves swishing sound like discouraged sighs or barely understood whispers. i hug trees. they have heartbeats, care for each other, have a circadian rhythm   and breathe
and breathe
and breathe
and breathe
and breathe
and breathe
and breathe

here i am on again about *these Black people*
another indignation caught
on camera   proof
and not enough

anyway
i want to write about the birds trilling
outside the kitchen window   i imagine
an argument   spirited discussion among
sparrows   a bright-yellow
bird i saw dip
fly around the blackberry bush

how the smell of spring grass tickles my nose
i want to write about the things i don't have
time to observe   write about
other than
Black deaths

fragrances
remind me of easier times when
i could roll carefree in thick fresh-cut green
grass   stubby blades prick my back
as the blue sky spun out thick wool clouds
trees whispered and swayed in time to their lullabies
carried on hot prairie wind   dust and wheat
acrid asphalt

petrichor

electric air swollen purple   orange skies
hair on end at attention   high-alert drum
rolling thunder   wait   weight
        heaviness

stay away from windows unplug appliances turn off the lights

i wish these were the only warnings, the only
worries i wish
after the fat drops land on baked
sidewalks and the percussive light show ends

go dance   wild abandon while silver droplets
ornament thick braids
sluice skin
widen this thoracic
cage

part III

medi

cine

Reparative care requires a transformation in the way we hold, exchange, and interact with one another and the web of life.
 —**RUPA MARYA** and **RAJ PATEL**
  Inflamed: Deep Medicine and the Anatomy of Injustice (2021)

today i walk through our neighbour's orchard
he points out a variegated ornamental grass
a fruiting woody peony – the pods hold seeds
lima bean–green and large that will turn black he says

hands me a peach with a little
conspiratorial smile then a large fig soft
and my fingers imagine pulpy, melty insides

a mulberry slyly handed
as i reach for a sweet green plum
bursting sweetness

points out a Spartan apple tree and a
hazelnut tree raccoons have feasted on
a fig tree nibbled by deer he says laughingly

i muse on how obsessively i used to wash
store-bought fruit soaking them in concoctions
of ACV or ocean-salty water
now sweet nectar from unwashed fruit
undulating down my throat

it rains – we've longed desperately for it
my bones neither portend nor divine its arrival
they've muted their protests to a dull
and rare flare-up so i am pleasantly surprised

at the wet whisper and murmur of water on
parched soil   petrichor and a summer of hellfire
commingle in the cooled night

crickets are not as loud as on dry hot nights

pleasantly surprised that i am not sob-walking
to a hellscape or an appointment or through life
pelvis tightened against threats real – imagined

a shield a barrier that has failed at a job
it was not meant to do

so it rains – the smell of parched life, thirst
slaked and a hope of dampening these hot spring
seasons, fall, and the inevitable Narnian winters

our breathless oceans
signal alarming climate change
that anxiety pales in comparison to the day-to-day

weather patterns

my body's a war zone
strategizing and plotting where to lob
its stabbing weapons

i'm at war with my body pretending to be neutral

tell myself to touch grass as a reminder to ground
myself   check in with the natural world
i touch grass often now – grows in wild profusion
smell rain and look

at jewelled spiderwebs glinting luxuriously
in the sun   water pearls
diamond bright

he has beautiful flowering trees this elder neighbour
one time he dropped by with fresh-caught
salmon
sweet sun-ripe plums and plump fragrant
blackberries
purple mulberries that stain
lips and fingers
in my previous life i scheduled acquaintances
and loved ones
like appointments – i couldn't handle spontaneity
and here a neighbour
happily unknowingly interrupts a work Zoom call
to hand me
this bounty of local seafood and fruit

in the morning i listen to the loudness of life
the now-familiar sound of the little red hummingbird
you can hear nearly a mile away long before
it zips by eye-level wings motor-like
sound mooing drifts from the valley

sometimes guests come over, used to
shrill sounds that
emanate from their screens
rapid-fire snippets
beat clips voice
over unnatural
speed robot tones
manufacture ear worms
multiply, mar
natural cacophony
slow rapid thousands of sound
their layered array
dizzy-making

displacing the stars
have you heard the sound of bird
wings flapping?
i arrive back in the city
farewell the sound of tree frogs
their mating disrupted by traffic noise
levels our endocrine systems too – disrupted
towards diabetes
the effect of these city-white lights
we're indifferent to
colonizing the night
brighter
blue light scattered, goodbye dark sky

i come from a family of farmers
on both sides of my family's tree, my parents and grandparents grew maize, coffee, peanuts, and other provisions. they sold these in the market for income, but also grew them for their day-to-day subsistence. my maternal grandfather ran a store where he sold what they grew, roasted the corn, peanuts, and coffee and sold them, ground, by weight. both sets of grandparents had goats and chickens and raised pigs. they worked their not-quite-ancestral lands – a *stopover* – if you will, from the Atlantic slave trade – under American occupation, through presidential assassinations (over seventy heads of state since 1791, most of whom didn't serve a full term), imperialist interventions, gunboat diplomacy, etc., fled as a result.

first to Tiohtià:ke – *the place where the nations and the rivers come together and divide* – colonially known as the island of Montréal, then to Treaty 1 Territory – Winnipeg. i've come strangely full circle after being a *city gal, prairie gal,* and now west-coast-island gal. the irony of feeling a sense of home, *here* despite my previous assertion: *it's not the same ocean i know but ocean is / ocean and it's salty.* i'm in a complicated relationship with *this land borrowed far from another.*

i hold anxiety cradled like a child or a favourite plushy.

i read *HARROWINGS* while overturning soil on abandoned beds, violently hacking the blackberries back, burning piles of thorny, snake-thick vines. the blackberry bushes have invaded and colonized the beds and the surrounding soil, choking the male kiwi tree – also overgrown, its branches braiding beautifully as it drapes. slash through the uneasiness – on this soil that i tell people is home – *here*. the three goats i've inherited browse nearby on the blackberry bushes that we haven't gotten to. later they will sit contentedly, stare, regurgitate their earlier meal.

i don't know a lot about farming despite my lineage, but we've been cultivating, growing, and canning for the past four years. the ongoing pandemic a catalyst that moved us from casual cultivating to subsistence farming. we canned last summer's bounty, which got us through our first hard winter. there are no canning recipes for the foods we enjoy, the ones we trial and error. Haitian sos pwa, Punjabi saag, Iranian khoresht e bademjan.

where have I been a settler is where I am
restored *returning to efforts of cultivation*

my dark brown fingers dig in soil. i watch all manner of bugs scuttle, even a little two-headed lizard. guilt's sharp sting at my having disrupted their home. my nails, *expensive city* nails a holdover from a summer wedding, are impractical for the task of growing and living off the land. it is *where i am restored.* shift soil, pull up weeds, drag wood for piling, drying. preparation for winter.

☙❧

on this rocky island colloquially named The Rock, more recently acknowledged as Xwe'etay a Coast Salish name (yew tree). instead of being in the war zone of street sweeps, state-funded genocides, my hands grip soil, caress velvety verdant grass, feet bared in still-frozen soil. wonder will we have enough rain when the stream evaporates, once the sun's arms lengthen, once the frogs stop singing their mating calls, once the feral lambs become grown? i still worry about women dying, staff mental health, the constant violence that backgrounds us all, some more than others, and the state's constant capitalist and carceral imposition on lives deemed worthless. i asked for a reprieve – my anxieties have shifted – but there is no ocean crossing wide enough to prevent violence seeping throughout.

on a call with my family doctor, he exclaims in his decade long plus of my being his patient, he's never seen me look so *light*. muses that maybe he should prescribe remote living for his patients and himself. i tell him about ParRX, the BC Parks Foundation and medical practitioners initiative connecting patients to nature.[1] i don't mention that this prescription relies on privilege – the access to a doctor – a good doctor at that. or the ability to access land. the irony of being prescribed stolen nature reserves. the privilege of not being in the middle of constant *harrowing*. my own privilege at some sort of *escape*.

---

[1] PaRx, an initiative of the BC Parks Foundation and driven by health-care professionals, is Canada's first national, evidence-based nature prescription program. The goal of PaRx is to promote prescribing time in nature for lifelong health benefit. www.parkprescriptions.ca/.

*... soil
is a great teacher in the fray*

a surface-deep practice of harrowing matters

this soil i grasp teaches me daily, regulates my nervous system, catches what leaks as gratitude despite the harrowing we encounter, despite the harrowing i've put this soil thru.

SOURCES

"[get ready]"
Tinush. "Struggle," featuring Aretha Franklin. Astrx ASTRXCD175, 2018.

"i read *goop*"
Rigden, Mia. "Nutrition and Lifestyle Tips to Manage Stress." *goop*. Accessed June 4, 2024. goop.com/ca-en/wellness/health/best-ways-to-manage-stress/.

"resignation letter with help from Hillary Leftwich and Sade"
Leftwich, Hillary (@hillary.leftwich). "Most of these posts are boring, I get it." Instagram post. January 14, 2023. www.instagram.com/p/CnZmu4rO4O9/?img_index=1.
Adu, Sade, Stuart Matthewman, Andrew Hale, and Paul S. Denman. "King of Sorrow." Track 3 on Sade, *Lovers Rock*. Epic 500766 2, 2000.

"Coping Like John Henry"
James, Sherman A. "John Henryism and the Health of African-Americans." *Culture, Medicine, and Psychiatry* 18, no. 2 (1994): 163–182. doi:10.1007/BF01379448.

"Patient Health Questionnaire"
Spitzer, Robert L., Janet B.W. Williams, Kurt Kroenke, and colleagues. "Patient Health Questionnaire – 9 (PHQ-9)." Accessed June 6, 2024. www.phqscreeners.com/images/sites/g/files/g10060481/f/201412/PHQ-9_English.pdf.

"displacing the stars"
Mortillaro, Nicole. "Goodbye, dark sky. The stars are rapidly disappearing from our night sky." *CBC*. Updated January 21, 2023. www.cbc.ca/news/science/light-pollution-increasing-1.6719034.

"i come from a family of farmers"
Désil, Junie. *eat salt | gaze at the ocean*. Vancouver: Talonbooks, 2020.
Nicholson, Cecily. *HARROWINGS*. Vancouver: Talonbooks, 2022.

ACKNOWLEDGMENTS

Gratitude to the highest.

Dearest Hari Alluri – I could not have completed this project without your support, dedicated editing, and the continual encouragement you offered. Your late-night efforts and inspiration helped me bring this collection to fruition. I am forever grateful.

My deepest thanks go to Catriona Strang for your incredible kindness and unwavering patience. Your support has been invaluable. To Kevin Williams and everyone at Talonbooks, thank you for making a home for my work. Your belief in me means the world.

A special thank you to Leslie Smith for his beautiful design work and for going well above and beyond to remake "do not circulate" in an even better format than the original. To Natasha Sanders-Kay and Fatima Amarshi – retreat partners, friends, collaborators, and cheerleaders extraordinaire – thank you for keeping it real. I eagerly anticipate the day your books grace the world.

Thank you to Christine Leviczky Riek and David Riek, whose beautiful home provided a serene retreat space where parts of this manuscript were written. Your generosity is greatly appreciated.

A heartfelt thank you to Joseph Kakwinokanasum, Brandon Wint, and Paolo Marcazzan for your contributions and encouragement. And to Jen Currin for your check-ins and ongoing support – always.

To my contemporaries in the poetry world – those who are pushing boundaries and reshaping the genre – you are a continual source of inspiration.

I am deeply thankful to my family for their boundless love and support throughout this journey.

I wrote "i come from a family of farmers" for the inaugural Phyllis Webb Memorial Reading at SFU. Thanks to the sponsors and organizers. Lastly, I extend my sincere appreciation to the Canada Council for the Arts for the grant that supported the creation of this manuscript.

If I have missed you in the acknowledgments, it is not intentional.

With gratitude.

Portions of *allostatic load* appeared in slightly modified forms in the following publications: *The Capilano Review*, *Capitalism Nature Socialism*, *The Spectacle*, *Loose Lips Magazine*, and *Canadian Literature*. Thanks to the editors.